DWELLING IN GOD'S PEACE

Jesus Calling Bible Study Series

JESUS CALLING® BIBLE STUDY SERIES

DWELLING IN GOD'S PEACE

EIGHT SESSIONS

with Karen Lee-Thorp

HarperChristian
Resources

CONTENTS

CONTENTS

INTRODUCTION

Sometimes our busy and difficult lives give us the impression that God is silent. We cry out to Him, but our feelings tell us that He isn't answering our prayers. In this, our feelings are incorrect. God hears the prayers of His children and speaks right into the situations in which we find ourselves. The trouble is that our lives are often too hectic, our minds too distracted, for us to take in what He offers.

This *Jesus Calling* Bible study is designed to help individuals and groups meditate on the words of Scripture and hear them not just as words said to people long ago but as words said to us today in the here and now. The goal is to help the heart open up and respond to what the mind reads—to encounter the living God as He speaks through the Scriptures. The writer to the Hebrews tells us:

> In the past God spoke to our ancestors through the prophets at many times and in various ways, but in these last days he has spoken to us by his Son, whom he appointed heir of all things, and through whom also he made the universe. The Son is the radiance of God's glory and the exact representation of his being, sustaining all things by his powerful word.
>
> —Hebrews 1:1–3

God has spoken to us through His Son, Jesus Christ. The New Testament gives us the chance to walk with Jesus, see what He does, and hear Him speak into the sometimes confusing situations in which we find ourselves. The Old Testament tells us the story of how God prepared a people to be the family of Jesus, and in the experiences of those men and women we find our own lives mirrored.

The Goal of This Series

The *Jesus Calling Bible Study Series* offers you a chance to lay down your cares, enter God's Presence, and hear Him speak through His Word. You will get to spend some time silently studying a passage of Scripture, and then, if you're meeting with a group, openly sharing your insights and hearing what others discovered. You'll also get to discuss excerpts from the *Jesus Calling* devotional that relate to the themes of the Bible passages. In this way, you will learn how to better make space in your life for the Spirit of God to speak to you through the Word of God and the people of God.

The Flow of Each Session

Each session of this study guide contains the following elements:

- Consider It. The two questions in this opening section serve as an icebreaker to help you start thinking about the theme of the session, connecting it to your own past or present experience and allowing you to get to know the others in your group more deeply. If you've had a busy day and your mind is full of distractions, these questions can help you better focus.

- EXPERIENCE IT. Here you will find two readings from *Jesus Calling* along with some questions for reflection. This is your chance to talk with others about the biblical principles found within the *Jesus Calling* devotions. Can you relate to what each reading describes? What insights from God's Word does it illuminate? What does it motivate you to do? This section will assist you in applying these biblical principles to your everyday habits.

- STUDY IT. Next you'll explore a Scripture passage connected to the session topic and the readings from *Jesus Calling.* You will not only analyze these Bible passages but also pray through them in ways designed to engage your heart and your head. You'll first talk with your group about what the verse or verses mean and then spend several minutes in silence, letting God speak into your life through His Word.

- LIVE IT. Finally, you will find five days' worth of suggested Scripture passages that you can pray through on your own during the week. Suggested questions for additional study and reflection are provided.

FOR LEADERS

If you are leading a group through this study guide, please see the Leader's Notes at the end of the guide. You'll find background on the design of the study as well as suggested answers for some of the study questions.

GOD'S PEACE
THROUGH FAITH
IN CHRIST

CONSIDER IT

If we were to name the things we most long for in life, peace would likely be at the top of the list for many of us. We desire love and joy as well—but the abiding sense of well-being called peace is something we crave in a world filled with experiences that make us anxious. In the Bible, peace is not primarily a feeling but a state that results from a rightly ordered relationship with God. We need peace with God, and feeling peaceful in our circumstances is a by-product of that relationship. Jesus is the One who has taken the initiative to bring about that peace. As we'll see in this first session, we receive this gift of peace when we respond with faith to what He has done for us.

1. *On a scale of 0 to 5, how peaceful would you describe your childhood? Why did you choose the number you did?*

0	1	2	3	4	5

Not at all peaceful   Supremely peaceful

_____

_____

2. *How peaceful is your life now? To what do you attribute that?*

0	1	2	3	4	5

Not at all peaceful   Supremely peaceful

_____

_____

EXPERIENCE IT

"My Peace is the treasure of treasures: *the pearl of great price.* It is an exquisitely costly gift, both for the Giver and the receiver. I purchased this Peace for you with My blood. You receive this gift by trusting Me in the midst of life's storms. If you have the world's peace—everything going your way—you don't seek My unfathomable Peace. Thank Me when things do not go your way, because spiritual blessings come wrapped in trials. Adverse circumstances are normal in a fallen world. Expect them each day. Rejoice in the face of hardship, *for I have overcome the world.*"

—FROM *JESUS CALLING,* JANUARY 24

3. *What does it mean that Jesus purchased His peace for you with His blood? Why was this even necessary?*

4. *Do you tend to think of adverse circumstances as normal—what anyone can expect as a part of life on this earth—or as surprises and outrages? Why did you answer the way you did?*

"*Peace be with you!* Ever since the resurrection, this has been My watchword to those who yearn for Me. As you sit quietly, let My Peace settle over you and enfold you in My loving Presence. To provide this radiant Peace for you, I died a criminal's death. Receive *My Peace* abundantly and thankfully. It is a rare treasure, dazzling in delicate beauty, yet strong enough to withstand all onslaughts. Wear My Peace with regal dignity. It will keep your heart and mind close to Mine."

—FROM *JESUS CALLING*, FEBRUARY 13

5. *How does it affect you to realize that Jesus, who never sinned, died a criminal's death (on a cross) to provide His peace for you?*

_____

_____

_____

6. *If you are a follower of Jesus, how easy is it for you to sit quietly and receive His peace? Why do you suppose this is the case?*

_____

_____

_____

STUDY IT

Read aloud the following passage from Romans 5:1–2, 6–11. Here, the apostle Paul explains that our right relationship with God has been restored through our faith in Jesus, who died to make it possible. As sinners, we were objects of God's holy wrath against sin, but now that Jesus has paid the price of our sin, we have peace with God.

4

[1] Therefore, since we have been justified through faith, we have peace with God through our Lord Jesus Christ, [2] through whom we have gained access by faith into this grace in which we now stand. And we boast in the hope of the glory of God. . . .

[6] You see, at just the right time, when we were still powerless, Christ died for the ungodly. [7] Very rarely will anyone die for a righteous person, though for a good person someone might possibly dare to die. [8] But God demonstrates his own love for us in this: While we were still sinners, Christ died for us.

[9] Since we have now been justified by his blood, how much more shall we be saved from God's wrath through him! [10] For if, while we were God's enemies, we were reconciled to him through the death of his Son, how much more, having been reconciled, shall we be saved through his life! [11] Not only is this so, but we also boast in God through our Lord Jesus Christ, through whom we have now received reconciliation.

7. *Why is peace with God foundational to all true feelings of peace?*

8. *What role does faith in Jesus play in restoring a relationship of peace with God?*

9. *Paul speaks of reconciliation in verse 10. What does reconciliation with God have to do with peace with God?*

_____

_____

_____

_____

10. *How have you experienced peace with God? What is it like for you? If you haven't experienced it, what is the lack of peace with Him like for you?*

_____

_____

_____

_____

11. *Take two minutes of silence to reread the passage, looking for a sentence, phrase, or even one word that stands out as something Jesus may want you to focus on in your life. If you're meeting with a group, the leader will keep track of time. At the end of two minutes, you may share with the group the word or phrase that came to you in the silence.*

_____

_____

_____

12. *Read the passage aloud again. Take another two minutes of silence, prayerfully considering what response God might want you to make to what you have read in His Word. If you're meeting with a group, the leader will again keep track of time. At the end of two minutes, you may share with the group what came to you in the silence if you wish.*

---

13. *If you're meeting with a group, how can the members pray for you? If you're using this study on your own, what would you like to say to God right now?*

LIVE IT

At the end of each session you'll find suggested Scripture readings for spending time alone with God during five days of the coming week. This week, the theme of each reading will focus on receiving God's peace. Read each passage slowly, pausing to think about what is being said. Rather than approaching this as an assignment to complete, think of it as an opportunity to meet with the One who loves you most. Use any of the questions that are helpful.

Day 1

Read Numbers 6:23–26. What does it mean to have the Lord "bless you and keep you"?

_____

_____

_____

Imagine the Lord with His face shining on you. How does this affect you?

_____

_____

_____

Why is it important to know that peace is a blessing God offers to His children, not something people devise by their own efforts?

_____

_____

_____

Consider memorizing these verses so you can reflect on God blessing you in this way and so you can offer this blessing to others.

Day 2

Read Psalm 4:8. What helps you sleep well? What, if anything, disturbs your sleep?

What reason for peaceful sleep does this verse offer?

Does this reason for peaceful sleep make a difference to you? If so, how? If not, what could you change in your life so that this verse offers you reassurance?

If you sleep well, give thanks to Jesus for this gift. If you don't, ask the Lord to help you know that in Him you dwell in complete safety.

Day 3

Read Psalm 29:3–11. How does the psalmist portray the Lord in verses 3–9?

_____

_____

_____

_____

How do you respond to this picture of God? What does it make you think, feel, and want to do?

_____

_____

_____

_____

What's your response to the idea that the Lord blesses His people with peace (verse 11)? Is this surprising? Why does it make sense?

_____

_____

_____

Praise the Lord of peace for being so powerful. Say to Him whatever the Holy Spirit might prompt you to say after reading this psalm.

Day 4

Read Psalm 34:11–14. Why is it important to keep your tongue from evil? What sorts of evil uses of the tongue do you think the psalmist wants you to avoid?

_____

_____

_____

_____

Even though peace is a blessing from God, the psalmist urges every believer to pursue it. How do you go about pursuing peace?

_____

_____

_____

_____

What does pursuing peace have to do with "rightly fearing" (taking seriously) the Lord?

_____

_____

_____

Today, look for ways to pursue peace—especially peace with other people.

Day 5

Read Psalm 85:8–9. To whom does the Lord promise peace? How would you say this in your own words?

_____

_____

_____

_____

What is folly? Why is it important to avoid it?

_____

_____

_____

Here again we see the fear of the Lord in the same passage as a promise of peace. How does fearing (taking seriously) the Lord help Christians gain His peace?

_____

_____

_____

Pay attention to any ways you are tempted to folly. Ask the Lord to help you overcome these temptations.

GOD'S PEACE
THROUGH OBEDIENCE
TO CHRIST

CONSIDER IT

In the "Live It" section for Session 1, you may have noticed a connection between peace and the fear of the Lord. Peace comes when we take the Lord seriously rather than taking Him for granted. This week, you will go deeper into that theme, studying verses that show how Jesus linked *loving Him*, *obeying Him*, and *experiencing peace*. Obedience doesn't need to be a scary subject. Remember, the Lord whom we are obeying is our beloved—the One who has our best interests at heart. He will never ask us to do something that is contrary to our own good.

1. *When you were a child, how inclined were you to obey your parents? Did you tend to be a fairly compliant child, or were you more strong-willed? Explain.*

2. *Would you describe your parents as strong disciplinarians or more permissive? What are some reasons for answering as you did?*

Experience It

"Learn to live from your true Center in Me. I reside in the deepest depths of your being, in eternal union with your spirit. It is at this deep level that My Peace reigns continually. You will not find lasting peace in the world around you, in circumstances, or in human relationships. The external world is always in flux—under the curse of death and decay. But there is a gold mine of Peace deep within you, waiting to be tapped. Take time to delve into the riches of My residing Presence. I want you to live increasingly from your real Center, where My Love has an eternal grip on you. *I am Christ in you, the hope of Glory.*"

—From *Jesus Calling*, February 20

3. *Do you have a "true Center" in Jesus, where you're united with Him and focused on Him? What helps you with this? What gets in the way?*

_____

_____

_____

_____

4. *In what ways have you experienced the truth that you will not find lasting peace in circumstances or human relationships? Why do you suppose this is the case?*

_____

_____

_____

"Try to view each day as an adventure, carefully planned out by your Guide. Instead of staring into the day that is ahead of you, attempting to program it according to your will, be attentive to Me and to all I have prepared for you. Thank Me for this day of life, recognizing that it is a precious, unrepeatable gift. Trust that I am with you each moment, whether you sense My Presence or not. A thankful, trusting attitude helps you to see events in your life from My perspective.

"A life lived close to Me will never be dull or predictable. Expect each day to contain surprises! Resist your tendency to search for the easiest route through the day. Be willing to follow wherever I lead. No matter how steep or treacherous the path before you, the safest place to be is by My side."

—FROM *JESUS CALLING*, JANUARY 13

5. *What are some of the ways you try to "program" your day according to your will? How have you found peace as you relinquished the control to Jesus?*

_____

_____

_____

6. *What is it like to walk closely with Jesus, listening for His directives in Scripture and following His lead? In what ways have you experienced this since you accepted Him as Savior?*

_____

_____

_____

STUDY IT

Read aloud the following passage from John 14:23–27. Note that Jesus offered these words of counsel to His disciples shortly before His arrest and execution. He is speaking of peace in the context of love and obedience.

[23] Jesus replied, "Anyone who loves me will obey my teaching. My Father will love them, and we will come to them and make our home with them. [24] Anyone who does not love me will not obey my teaching. These words you hear are not my own; they belong to the Father who sent me.

[25] "All this I have spoken while still with you. [26] But the Advocate, the Holy Spirit, whom the Father will send in my name, will teach you all things and will remind you of everything I have said to you. [27] Peace I leave with you; my peace I give you. I do not give to you as the world gives. Do not let your hearts be troubled and do not be afraid."

7. *Why is it that anyone who truly loves Jesus will also obey Him?*

8. *What do we learn about the Holy Spirit from this passage? What is His role in guiding us?*

9. *How would you describe the connection between obedience, which Jesus talks about at the beginning of this passage, and peace, which He talks about at the end?*

_____

_____

_____

_____

10. *Why do you think Jesus says, "I do not give to you as the world gives"? What does the world give? What does Jesus give that is different?*

_____

_____

_____

_____

11. *Take two minutes of silence to reread the passage, looking for a sentence, phrase, or even one word that stands out as something Jesus may want you to focus on in your life. If you're meeting with a group, the leader will keep track of time. At the end of two minutes, you may share with the group the word or phrase that came to you in the silence.*

_____

_____

_____

12. *Read the passage aloud again. Take two minutes of silence, asking Jesus what He is saying to you through the word or phrase you selected and whether He would like you to do anything in response. If you're meeting with a group, the leader will again keep track of time. At the end of two minutes, you may share with the group what came to you in the silence if you wish.*

13. *If you're meeting with a group, how can the members pray for you? If you're using this study on your own, what would you like to say to God right now?*

LIVE IT

This week's daily Scripture readings focus on having the kind of obedience that leads to peace. Read each passage slowly, pausing to think about what is being said. Rather than approaching this as an assignment to complete, think of it as an opportunity to meet with a Person. Use any of the questions that are helpful.

Day 1

Read Psalm 103:17–20. What does the psalmist say about obedience to the Lord?

_____

_____

_____

_____

The psalmist writes that even the angels "do his bidding" (verse 20). What does this say about peace in God's kingdom? What does this say to you about your own obedience?

_____

_____

_____

In what particular area of your life is God calling you to obedience today? How is He guiding you in your current situation?

_____

_____

_____

Praise Jesus for His guidance, which leads to the way of peace for those who obey it.

Day 2

Read Psalm 119:33–35. How easy is it for you to imagine finding delight in obeying Jesus' commands? Why is that the case?

Why is it important to obey with all your heart—not grudgingly?

How can you see yourself finding peace by following Jesus' guidance for you today?

Pray for Jesus to teach you the way of His decrees today.

Day 3

Read Matthew 28:18–20. Jesus issued these words, called the "Great Commission," just before He ascended into heaven after His resurrection. What does Jesus promise in this passage? What does He require of His disciples?

_____

_____

_____

Why is it not possible to claim Jesus' promise in this passage without following His command?

_____

_____

_____

If you are a follower of Christ, how are you actively heeding this command today? What are some things, if any, that have gotten in the way?

_____

_____

_____

Thank Jesus for giving all believers a role in His Great Commission. Ask Him to help you accept that role, fulfill His command, and find peace in obedience today.

Day 4

Read Luke 11:27–28. Why do you suppose Jesus didn't just say "thank you" for the blessing the woman called out?

Does it surprise you that Jesus attaches a blessing to hearing and obeying rather than to something else, like believing? Explain.

How willing are you to hear and obey what God asks you to do—even if it is difficult? Does it seem like a life-giving thing to do or just drudgery? Why?

Embrace Jesus' blessing today by committing to obey Him. Thank Him for the peace that He provides when you follow His commands.

Day 5

Read Romans 6:16–18. What do you think the apostle Paul means by the phrase "slaves of righteousness" (verse 18)?

_____

_____

_____

_____

How can you be a slave of righteousness? Why would you want to be?

_____

_____

_____

How does a person move from being a "slave to sin" to a "slave to righteousness"? What role does obedience to God play in the process?

_____

_____

_____

Thank Jesus today for allowing you the opportunity to be His joyful slave to righteousness.

GOD'S PEACE THROUGH THE WORK OF THE HOLY SPIRIT

CONSIDER IT

We are often quicker to understand what we read in the Bible about Jesus because we know that He became a human being like us and was willing to die on our behalf. We tend to be less clear on who the Holy Spirit is, what He is like, and the role He plays in the lives of Christ followers. However, as we discussed in the last session, the Holy Spirit is the Advocate the Father sent to help believers move through this life in love, obedience, and peace. If we want to lead the lives that God intends for us, it's important to better understand the Spirit's role.

In this session, we will look more closely at how our peace is rooted in the Holy Spirit's Presence and who He is according to Scripture. We will also find assurance that, if we have accepted Jesus as our Savior, the Holy Spirit is always with us and in us, just as surely as Christ lived among us. The more connected we are with the Spirit of God, the more peace from God we will experience in our lives.

1. *What are your perceptions of the Holy Spirit? How do you tend to view Him?*

_____

_____

_____

_____

2. *What has brought you peace or a lack of peace in your day today?*

_____

_____

_____

EXPERIENCE IT

"Understanding will never bring you Peace. That's why I have instructed you to *trust in Me, not in your understanding*. Human beings have a voracious appetite for trying to figure things out in order to gain a sense of mastery over their lives. But the world presents you with an endless series of problems. As soon as you master one set, another pops up to challenge you. The relief you had anticipated is short-lived. Soon your mind is gearing up again: searching for understanding (mastery), instead of seeking Me (your Master).

"The wisest of all men, Solomon, could never think his way through to Peace. His vast understanding resulted in feelings of futility, rather than in fulfillment. Finally, he lost his way and succumbed to the will of his wives by worshiping idols.

"My Peace is not an elusive goal, hidden at the center of some complicated maze. Actually, you are always enveloped in Peace, which is inherent in My Presence. As you look to Me, you gain awareness of this precious Peace."

—FROM *JESUS CALLING*, AUGUST 7

3. *What is the problem with seeking understanding so we can feel in control of every situation? How does the Holy Spirit play a role in giving believers the understanding they truly need?*

_____

_____

_____

_____

4. *In Galatians 5:22 we read that peace is a fruit of the Spirit that God provides to His children. How does the Holy Spirit make believers aware of Jesus' precious peace? What role do we, as Christians, play in seeking that peace?*

_____

_____

_____

"I am involved in each moment of your life. I have carefully mapped out every inch of your journey through this day, even though much of it may feel haphazard. Because the world is in a fallen condition, things always seem to be unraveling around the edges. Expect to find trouble in this day. At the same time, trust that My way is perfect, even in the midst of such messy imperfection.

"Stay conscious of Me as you go through this day, remembering that I never leave your side. Let the Holy Spirit guide you step by step, protecting you from unnecessary trials and equipping you to get through whatever must be endured. As you trudge through the sludge of this fallen world, keep your mind in heavenly places with Me. Thus the Light of My Presence shines on you, giving you Peace and Joy that circumstances cannot touch."

—FROM *JESUS CALLING*, JUNE 1

5. *What do you do to keep your mind focused on God so you can see where the Holy Spirit is guiding your Christian walk step by step? What do you struggle with when you try to be still?*

_____

_____

6. *The apostle Paul writes that believers should "take captive every thought to make it obedient to Christ" (2 Corinthians 10:5). In what ways do you ask the Holy Spirit to help you take control of your thoughts? What does this look like in your life?*

Study It

Read aloud the following passage from Romans 8:5–11. In these verses, Paul talks about two ways your mind can be focused: (1) on what the flesh desires, or (2) on what the Holy Spirit desires. Note that when Paul mentions *flesh*, he doesn't mean the body or sexual sin. Rather, he is referring to the human condition in which Jesus and the Holy Spirit are ignored. Paul means thinking or living in this narrowly human way.

[5] Those who live according to the flesh have their minds set on what the flesh desires; but those who live in accordance with the Spirit have their minds set on what the Spirit desires. [6] The mind governed by the flesh is death, but the mind governed by the Spirit is life and peace. [7] The mind governed by the flesh is hostile to God; it does not submit to God's law, nor can it do so. [8] Those who are in the realm of the flesh cannot please God.

[9] You, however, are not in the realm of the flesh but are in the realm of the Spirit, if indeed the Spirit of God lives in you. And if anyone does not have the Spirit of Christ, they do not belong to Christ. [10] But if Christ is in you, then even though your body is subject to death because of sin, the Spirit gives life because of righteousness. [11] And if the Spirit of him who raised Jesus from the dead is living in you, he who raised

Christ from the dead will also give life to your mortal bodies because of his Spirit who lives in you.

7. *What are some of the things the flesh desires (other than sex)? What are some human desires we have when we ignore Jesus and the Holy Spirit?*

_____

_____

_____

_____

8. *What are some of the things the Holy Spirit desires?*

_____

_____

_____

_____

9. *Given these two very different sets of desires, why do you suppose life and peace come only to those who set their minds on the things the Spirit desires?*

_____

_____

_____

10. *What should foster peace in our hearts, according to verses 9–11?*

11. *Take two minutes of silence to reread the passage, looking for a sentence, phrase, or even one word that stands out as something Jesus may want you to focus on in your life. If you're meeting with a group, the leader will keep track of time. At the end of two minutes, you may share with the group the word or phrase that came to you in the silence.*

12. *Read the passage aloud again. Take another two minutes of silence, prayerfully considering what response God might want you to make to what you have read in His Word. If you're meeting with a group, the leader will again keep track of time. At the end of two minutes, you may share with the group what came to you in the silence if you wish.*

13. *If you're meeting with a group, how can the members pray for you? If you're using this study on your own, what would you like to say to God right now?*

_____

_____

LIVE IT

The theme of this week's daily Scripture readings is on receiving peace through the work of the Holy Spirit in your life. Read each passage slowly, pausing to think about what is being said. Rather than approaching this as an assignment to complete, think of it as an opportunity to meet with a Person. Use any of the questions that are helpful.

Day 1

Read Galatians 5:13–15. What "freedom" is Paul referring to here? Why is it important for believers not to use this freedom to indulge their fleshly desires?

_____

_____

What opportunities do you have to serve others in love?

_____

_____

_____

What do you think Paul means in verse 15 by biting and devouring one another? Why is it so important to avoid this? How might such godly discipline promote peace?

Thank Jesus for giving you opportunities to serve others. Look for additional ways to serve today.

Day 2

Read Galatians 5:16–18. What does it mean to "walk by the Spirit" (verse 16)?

If you are a Christian, how can you walk by the Spirit today?

What is a fleshly desire that you need to put aside in order to live in the peace the Spirit offers?

Be on the lookout for ways to cultivate a greater awareness of Jesus as you move through your day—and be responsive if you get a nudge from the Holy Spirit to serve someone else.

Day 3

Read Galatians 5:19–21. How do the acts of the flesh lead away from peace?

_____

_____

_____

What does it mean to "live like this" (verse 21)? What is the end result for those who choose this path?

_____

_____

_____

How easy is it for you to avoid acts of the flesh? What helps you or gets in the way?

_____

_____

_____

_____

Ask Jesus today to help you embrace the work of the Spirit in your life and continually move away from the desires that lead to acts of the flesh.

Day 4

Read Galatians 5:22–23. Why do you think Paul calls these the fruit of the Spirit? What does calling them fruit tell you about these characteristics?

Where do you see the fruit of the Spirit in the lives of Christians you know? (Think especially of the fruit of peace.)

If you are a believer, where do you see the fruit of the Spirit in your own life? In what areas do you need to grow?

Thank God today for the fruit of the Spirit that He freely offers to those who choose to obey and follow His will.

Day 5

Read Galatians 5:24–26. How does a person crucify the flesh?

_____

_____

Once again, Paul emphasizes walking by the Spirit, or keeping "in step with the Spirit" (verse 25). Why do you think he makes a point of repeating this phrase?

_____

_____

_____

After reading all of Galatians 5, what have you learned about the connection between the Spirit and peace, or the connection between the flesh and the lack of peace?

_____

_____

_____

Pray throughout the day today to walk by the Spirit. Watch for opportunities.

GOD'S PEACE IN THE MIDST OF SUFFERING

CONSIDER IT

It's relatively easy to dwell in peace when everything is going well. It's much harder when things fall apart, when our loved ones suffer tragic loss or illness, or when we lose a job and see no prospect of getting another one in the immediate future. Anxiety hits hard during times of suffering—and it can be difficult to discern a way out. In this session, we will follow the story of a godly man in the Bible who learned a great deal about suffering in a short amount of time. We'll examine our own experiences of suffering and ask how we can have peace in the midst of them. And we will explore Jesus' promises to stick with us through adversity and ways that our peace actually grows more robust when it is tested by fire. No matter what storms come our way, Jesus never lets go of us.

1. *When you were growing up, how did your parents usually cope with hard times?*

_____

_____

_____

_____

2. *Why is it often difficult for even Christians to feel God's presence during times of suffering?*

_____

_____

_____

EXPERIENCE IT

"Receive *My Peace*. It is My continual gift to you. The best way to receive this gift is to sit quietly in My Presence, trusting Me in every area of your life. *Quietness and trust* accomplish far more than you can imagine: not only in you, but also on earth and in heaven. When you trust Me in a given area, you release that problem or person into My care.

"Spending time alone with Me can be a difficult discipline because it goes against the activity addiction of this age. You may appear to be doing nothing, but actually you are participating in battles going on within spiritual realms. You are waging war—not with *the weapons of the world*, but with heavenly weapons, which *have divine power to demolish strongholds*. Living close to Me is a sure defense against evil."

—FROM *JESUS CALLING*, SEPTEMBER 12

3. *How easy is it for you to sit quietly in Jesus' presence and receive His peace regardless of what you are facing? What would help you do this?*

4. *Have you ever considered that your quietness and trust in God could actually accomplish something in the spiritual realm? In what ways can this be true?*

"My Peace is like a shaft of golden Light shining on you continuously. During days of bright sunshine, it may blend in with your surroundings. On darker days, My Peace stands out in sharp contrast to your circumstances. See times of darkness as opportunities for My Light to shine in transcendent splendor. I am training you to practice Peace that overpowers darkness. Collaborate with Me in this training. *Do not grow weary and lose heart.*"

—FROM *JESUS CALLING*, FEBRUARY 11

5. *How does this reading speak of our experience of Jesus' peace on bright days and on dark days? How would you communicate this in your own words?*

_____

_____

_____

_____

6. *How can you go about practicing peace that overcomes the darkness?*

_____

_____

_____

STUDY IT

Read aloud the following passage from Job 1:1–22. This is a startling story in the Bible that gives us a glimpse into what goes on in the spiritual realms. It is also one of the first places in the Bible where the name Satan appears. The name means *Accuser* or *Adversary*.

¹ In the land of Uz there lived a man whose name was Job. This man was blameless and upright; he feared God and shunned evil. ² He had seven sons and three daughters, ³ and he owned seven thousand sheep, three thousand camels, five hundred yoke of oxen and five hundred donkeys, and had a large number of servants. He was the greatest man among all the people of the East.

⁴ His sons used to hold feasts in their homes on their birthdays, and they would invite their three sisters to eat and drink with them. ⁵ When a period of feasting had run its course, Job would make arrangements for them to be purified. Early in the morning he would sacrifice a burnt offering for each of them, thinking, "Perhaps my children have sinned and cursed God in their hearts." This was Job's regular custom.

⁶ One day the angels came to present themselves before the LORD, and Satan also came with them. ⁷ The LORD said to Satan, "Where have you come from?"

Satan answered the LORD, "From roaming throughout the earth, going back and forth on it."

⁸ Then the LORD said to Satan, "Have you considered my servant Job? There is no one on earth like him; he is blameless and upright, a man who fears God and shuns evil."

⁹ "Does Job fear God for nothing?" Satan replied. ¹⁰ "Have you not put a hedge around him and his household and everything he has? You have blessed the work of his hands, so that his flocks and herds are spread throughout the land. ¹¹ But now stretch out your hand and strike everything he has, and he will surely curse you to your face."

¹² The LORD said to Satan, "Very well, then, everything he has is in your power, but on the man himself do not lay a finger."

Then Satan went out from the presence of the LORD.

¹³ One day when Job's sons and daughters were feasting and drinking wine at the oldest brother's house, ¹⁴ a messenger came to Job and said, "The oxen were plowing and the donkeys were grazing nearby, ¹⁵ and the Sabeans attacked and made off with them. They put the servants to the sword, and I am the only one who has escaped to tell you!"

¹⁶ While he was still speaking, another messenger came and said, "The fire of God fell from the heavens and burned up the sheep and the servants, and I am the only one who has escaped to tell you!"

¹⁷ While he was still speaking, another messenger came and said, "The Chaldeans formed three raiding parties and swept down on your camels and made off with them. They put the servants to the sword, and I am the only one who has escaped to tell you!"

¹⁸ While he was still speaking, yet another messenger came and said, "Your sons and daughters were feasting and drinking wine at the oldest brother's house, ¹⁹ when suddenly a mighty wind swept in from the desert and struck the four corners of the house. It collapsed on them and they are dead, and I am the only one who has escaped to tell you!"

²⁰ At this, Job got up and tore his robe and shaved his head. Then he fell to the ground in worship ²¹ and said:

> "Naked I came from my mother's womb
>   and naked I will depart.
> THE LORD GAVE AND THE LORD HAS TAKEN AWAY;
>   may the name of the LORD be praised."

²² In all this, Job did not sin by charging God with wrongdoing.

7. *What accusation does Satan make in verses 9–11? How is God's glory at stake?*

_____

_____

_____

_____

_____

8. *Do you think God betrays Job by letting Satan test him? What can we learn from this passage about one possible reason why God might allow suffering in our lives?*

9. *Consider Job's response to the tragic news he receives (verses 20–22). What feelings and beliefs does he express?*

10. *Would you say that Job has learned to live his life trusting in God and walking in the peace that He provides each day? Why did you answer the way you did?*

11. *Take two minutes of silence to reread the passage, looking for a sentence, phrase, or even one word that stands out as something Jesus may want you to focus on in your life. If you're meeting with a group, the leader will keep track of time. At the end of two minutes, you may share with the group the word or phrase that came to you in the silence.*

_____

_____

_____

12. *Read the passage aloud again. Take another two minutes of silence, prayerfully considering what response God might want you to make to what you have read in His Word. If you're meeting with a group, the leader will again keep track of time. At the end of two minutes, you may share with the group what came to you in the silence if you wish.*

_____

_____

_____

13. *If you're meeting with a group, how can the members pray for you? If you're using this study on your own, what would you like to say to God right now?*

_____

_____

_____

LIVE IT

The theme of this week's daily Scripture readings is on how you can have peace in the midst of adversity. Read each passage slowly, pausing to think about what is being said. Rather than approaching this as an assignment to complete, think of it as an opportunity to meet with a Person. Use any of the questions that are helpful.

Day 1

Read Isaiah 30:19–21. How does God promise to respond to cries for help from His sons and daughters?

Why do you suppose it's such good news that the Lord will give His people teachers (verse 20)?

Does clear guidance (verse 21) help you have peace? Why is that the case?

Speak with God about your need for guidance. Cry to Him for help if you need it. Remember that He always responds to His children.

Day 2

Read Isaiah 26:3–4. What is a steadfast mind? How can you tell if your mind is steadfast?

Why do you think a steadfast mind is so important for peace?

Trust is key. What reasons for trusting the Lord do you have?

Talk with Jesus about your trust in Him. Ask Him to help you have a steadfast mind.

Day 3

Read Isaiah 32:16–20. This passage contrasts what will happen in the desert (a normally dangerous place because of its remoteness) with what happens in the city (typically a safer place in biblical times). What will life be like for the Lord's people in the desert (verses 16–18)? What will happen to the city (verse 19)?

Why do you suppose righteousness leads to peace for the people of God (verse 17)?

How can you cultivate righteousness in your own life?

_____

_____

_____

If you're in a desert place right now and are a child of God, thank the Lord for enabling you to have peace there. Take some quiet time just to rest in Jesus' Presence.

Day 4

Read Isaiah 53:4–6. This passage is about what Jesus has done for His followers. What has He done with our suffering? How aware of this are you?

_____

_____

_____

When the prophet speaks of "the punishment that brought us peace" in verse 5, what is he talking about? What is this peace that we have received?

_____

_____

_____

How does thinking about this passage help you to have peace as a child of God in the midst of hardship?

Thank Jesus for taking your punishment on Himself so that you could have peace. Ask Him to put a deep awareness of this generous gift into your heart so that you can know how good He is to you even when times are hard.

Day 5

Read Isaiah 54:10–15. Here the Lord is talking to Jerusalem, the capital city of His people, which has been demolished because of the people's sin. What does He promise His people in verse 10?

What other aspects of His promises in this passage are especially meaningful to you?

The Lord makes these promises, and yet circumstances don't necessarily get better quickly. What are we to draw from this? Why would He make promises and then require us to wait to see them fulfilled?

_____

_____

_____

Tell Jesus how you feel about waiting to see the fulfillment of His promises. Ask Him to give you the strength to hold onto peace in faith while you wait.

GOD'S PEACE AMONG BELIEVERS IN CHRIST

CONSIDER IT

As important as it is for us to have peace within ourselves as Christians, inner peace is not the only kind of peace referred to in the Bible. There are many passages that address living peaceably with other people—especially *other believers*. As we will see in this session, Jesus' sacrifice on the cross provides the means for us to be reconciled with God and to live at peace with each other. When we accept Jesus as our Lord and Savior, it opens the way for us to break down the barriers that divide people and truly love another. As preparation for this session, think about any relationships you have (particularly with other believers) that are less than whole and healthy. Allow Jesus to warm your heart to the possibility of having true peace with those people.

1. *When you disagree with another person, what is your typical means of dealing with it? Are you more inclined to argue, withdraw, talk it through calmly, or pretend nothing is wrong?*

2. *If you are a believer, what is something you would like to change as it relates to how you get along with your fellow brothers and sisters in Christ?*

EXPERIENCE IT

"Take time to *be still* in My Presence. The more hassled you feel, the more you need this sacred space of communion with Me. Breathe slowly and deeply. Relax in My holy Presence while *My Face shines upon you*. This is how you receive My Peace, which I always proffer to you.

"Imagine the pain I feel when My children tie themselves up in anxious knots, ignoring My gift of Peace. I died a criminal's death to secure this blessing for you. Receive it gratefully; hide it in your heart. My Peace is an inner treasure, growing within you as you trust in Me. Therefore, circumstances cannot touch it. Be still, enjoying Peace in My Presence."

—FROM *JESUS CALLING*, OCTOBER 13

3. *What are some of the benefits of being still in Jesus' presence—of simply relaxing when you are spending time with Him?*

_____

_____

_____

4. *How do you think it might affect Jesus when you tie yourself up in anxious knots?*

_____

_____

_____

"Come to Me, and rest in My Peace. My Face is shining upon you, in rays of *Peace transcending understanding*. Instead of trying to figure things out yourself, you can relax in the Presence of the One who knows everything. As you lean on Me in trusting dependence, you feel peaceful and complete. This is how I designed you to live: in close communion with Me.

"When you are around other people, you tend to cater to their expectations—real or imagined. You feel enslaved to pleasing them, and your awareness of My Presence grows dim. Your efforts to win their approval eventually exhaust you. You offer these people dry crumbs rather than the *living water* of My Spirit flowing through you. This is not My way for you! Stay in touch with Me, even during your busiest moments. Let My Spirit give you words of grace as you live in the Light of My Peace."

—FROM *JESUS CALLING*, NOVEMBER 18

5. *How closely do you identify with these words about relating to other people? Do you offer others "dry crumbs" rather than the "living water" of the Holy Spirit? Explain.*

_____

_____

_____

_____

6. *How can you stay in touch with Jesus even during your busiest moments and speak His words of grace to others?*

_____

_____

_____

Study It

Read aloud the following passage from Ephesians 2:11–22. In these verses, Paul is referring to the former hostility that existed between Jews and non-Jews (Gentiles). The church in Ephesus contained both Jews and Gentiles, and Paul wanted them to understand that Jesus was the reason they could—and *should*—get along with each other. The apostle speaks primarily to the Gentiles, who had not been included in the special (covenant) relationship that God had with the Jewish people. When Jesus came, He made life in God available to *anyone* who would believe in Him, so now *all* are included in that covenant—whether Jew or Gentile. For this reason, Paul states, divisions should not occur in the church, particularly those between different ethnic groups or factions.

[11] Therefore, remember that formerly you who are Gentiles by birth . . . [12] remember that at that time you were separate from Christ, excluded from citizenship in Israel and foreigners to the covenants of the promise, without hope and without God in the world. [13] But now in Christ Jesus you who once were far away have been brought near by the blood of Christ.

[14] For he himself is our peace, who has made the two groups one and has destroyed the barrier, the dividing wall of hostility, [15] by setting aside in his flesh the law with its commands and regulations. His purpose was to create in himself one new humanity out of the two, thus making peace, [16] and in one body to reconcile both of them to God through the cross, by which he put to death their hostility. [17] He came and preached peace to you who were far away and peace to those who were near. [18] For through him we both have access to the Father by one Spirit.

[19] Consequently, you are no longer foreigners and strangers, but fellow citizens with God's people and also members of his household, [20] built on the foundation of the apostles and prophets, with Christ Jesus himself as the chief cornerstone. [21] In him the whole building is joined together and rises to become a holy temple in the Lord. [22] And in him

you too are being built together to become a dwelling in which God lives by his Spirit.

7. *How does Paul describe the former state of the Gentiles (those who are not Jewish)?*

_____

_____

_____

_____

8. *What difference does it make that Jesus made it possible for people— regardless of their ethnic background—to live in peace with each other?*

_____

_____

_____

9. *Do you have a relationship that is fractured, causing you a lack of peace? If so, what is the dividing wall of hostility in that relationship?*

_____

_____

_____

10. *Paul wanted Jewish and Gentile believers to see themselves as fellow citizens of Jesus' kingdom and members of His household, His family. He wanted them to think of themselves as stones being put together into a single temple of the Lord. How can this motivate you to seek peace with those you've been avoiding or with those whom you find it hard to get along with? What is a step you can take toward peace?*

---

11. *Take two minutes of silence to reread the passage, looking for a sentence, phrase, or even one word that stands out as something Jesus may want you to focus on in your life. If you're meeting with a group, the leader will keep track of time. At the end of two minutes, you may share with the group the word or phrase that came to you in the silence.*

---

12. *Read the passage aloud again. Take another two minutes of silence, prayerfully considering what response God might want you to make to what you have read in His Word. If you're meeting with a group, the leader will again keep track of time. At the end of two minutes, you may share with the group what came to you in the silence if you wish.*

_____

_____

_____

_____

13. *If you're meeting with a group, how can the members pray for you? If you're using this study on your own, what would you like to say to God right now?*

_____

_____

_____

_____

LIVE IT

The theme of this week's daily Scripture readings is on the peace that God has brought to all believers in Christ by reconciling us to Himself. Read each passage slowly, pausing to think about what is being said. Rather than approaching this as an assignment to complete, think of it as an opportunity to meet with a Person. Use any of the questions that are helpful.

Day 1

Read Colossians 1:15. What do you think Paul means when he says that Jesus is "the image of the invisible God"?

_____

_____

_____

_____

What does it mean to call Jesus "the firstborn over all creation"?

_____

_____

_____

What difference does it make to you personally that these things are true of Jesus? How do they add to your peace?

_____

_____

_____

Spend some time today in silent worship of Jesus—the image of the invisible God and the firstborn over all creation.

Day 2

Read Colossians 1:16–17. Thrones, powers, rulers, and authorities refer to angelic powers and possibly earthly ones as well. What does this say about Jesus' authority over this world?

How does it affect you that all things were created through Jesus?

What difference does it make that the only way things hold together is in Jesus?

Praise and worship Jesus today for being the One through whom all things—including you and everything that belongs to you—are created and are held together.

Day 3

Read Colossians 1:18. Why is it important that Jesus is the head of the church, which is now His body on earth? How should this affect your relationships within the church?

What have you learned about Jesus in these verses in Colossians that can set your mind at peace when it is stirred with anxiety?

How will the truths you have learned in these verses affect your relationships with others?

Rest in Jesus' presence today, knowing that He is in control of everything in this world and has everything in your life under control.

Day 4

Read Colossians 1:19–20. What does it mean that God was pleased to have "all his fullness" dwell in Christ? How has He reconciled humans to Himself?

In your words, how would you describe the way Jesus makes peace through His shed blood with those who believe in Him?

How can you remember and experience that peace as you go through your day today?

If you are a follower of Christ, thank Him for reconciling you and everything else in the world to the Father. Thank Him for being the source of your peace.

Day 5

Read Colossians 1:21–23. In what ways do you identify with the description of your past in these verses?

What has God done for every believer through Jesus? What does this have to do with peace?

What does God ask His people to do in verse 23? What will that look like for you today?

If you have accepted Jesus as your Lord and Savior, look for an opportunity to stand firm in your faith in Him today. Choose to trust Jesus, who is your peace, in all the things you'll face.

GOD'S PEACE THROUGH THE PRACTICE OF PRAYER

CONSIDER IT

People in our world today are longing for the "secret" to inner peace. Our society promises this peace can be obtained through possessions (*you will be secure if you have enough wealth*) or relationships (*you will be happy if you just meet the right person*), or status (*you will be content if people respect you as someone of importance*). However, as we will examine in today's study, the Bible points us to a different source for finding true peace.

Ironically, the apostle Paul tells us about this "secret" from the confines of a prison cell. He has been arrested for disturbing the public's peace by preaching about Jesus, and there is a real possibility that he could be given a death sentence. He writes to a small band of believers in a town where he had been beaten and jailed for preaching about Jesus. These believers were probably not threatened with prison, but they had endured the scorn of their neighbors and likely discrimination as well. It was not at all easy to be a follower of Jesus in their town.

This is a man who knows the secret of peace, and these are the people with whom he shares it. It will not be the peace of an untroubled life. But it will be the kind of peace we need.

1. *What messages have you received from the world about what brings true peace? Give some specific examples.*

_____

_____

_____

_____

_____

2. *What are some things you do to find peace? On what do you focus when you need peace?*

_____

_____

_____

EXPERIENCE IT

"Peace is My continual gift to you. It flows abundantly from My throne of grace. Just as the Israelites could not store up manna for the future but had to gather it daily, so it is with My Peace. The day-by-day collecting of manna kept My people aware of their dependence on Me. Similarly, I give you sufficient Peace for the present when you come to me *by prayer and petition with thanksgiving.* If I gave you permanent Peace, independent of My Presence, you might fall into the trap of self-sufficiency. May that never be!

"I have designed you to need Me moment by moment. As your awareness of your neediness increases, so does your realization of My abundant sufficiency. *I can meet every one of your needs* without draining My resources at all. *Approach My throne of grace with bold confidence,* receiving My Peace with a thankful heart."

—FROM *JESUS CALLING*, APRIL 18

3. *Why is self-sufficiency a trap in our lives?*

_____

_____

_____

4. *How has awareness of your neediness increased your realization of God's abundant sufficiency in your life? Describe your experience.*

_____

_____

_____

"My Face is shining upon you, beaming out *Peace that transcends understanding.* You are surrounded by a sea of problems, but you are face to Face with Me, your Peace. As long as you focus on Me, you are safe. If you gaze too long at the myriad problems around you, you will sink under the weight of your burdens. When you start to sink, simply call out, "Help me, Jesus!" and I will lift you up.

"The closer you live to Me, the safer you are. Circumstances around you are undulating, and there are treacherous-looking waves in the distance. *Fix your eyes on Me,* the One who never changes. By the time those waves reach you, they will have shrunk to proportions of My design. I am always beside you, helping you face *today's* waves. The future is a phantom, seeking to spook you. Laugh at the future! Stay close to Me."

—FROM *JESUS CALLING,* JANUARY 15

5. *How does it help you to know that even in a sea of problems, you are always face-to-Face with God if you belong to Him?*

_____

_____

_____

6. *What are some things that God calls His children to do to deal with their problems?*

_____

_____

_____

STUDY IT

Read aloud the following passage from Philippians 4:4–13. As mentioned previously, Paul wrote this letter to the believers in Philippi from a jail cell. It is likely the Philippians had become disheartened by the news of this imprisonment, and Paul wished to explain to them the significance of it in light of the work he was doing for Christ. Even though death was staring him in the face, he would choose to rejoice in what Jesus had done for him—and he wanted the Philippians to follow his example.

[4] Rejoice in the Lord always. I will say it again: Rejoice! [5] Let your gentleness be evident to all. The Lord is near. [6] Do not be anxious about anything, but in every situation, by prayer and petition, with thanksgiving, present your requests to God. [7] And the peace of God, which transcends all understanding, will guard your hearts and your minds in Christ Jesus.

[8] Finally, brothers and sisters, whatever is true, whatever is noble, whatever is right, whatever is pure, whatever is lovely, whatever is admirable—if anything is excellent or praiseworthy—think about such things. [9] Whatever you have learned or received or heard from me, or seen in me—put it into practice. And the God of peace will be with you.

[10] I rejoiced greatly in the Lord that at last you renewed your concern for me. Indeed, you were concerned, but you had no opportunity to show it. [11] I am not saying this because I am in need, for I have learned

to be content whatever the circumstances. [12] I know what it is to be in need, and I know what it is to have plenty. I have learned the secret of being content in any and every situation, whether well fed or hungry, whether living in plenty or in want. [13] I can do all this through him who gives me strength.

7. *The believers in Philippi were undergoing discrimination because of their faith, and yet Paul instructed them to "rejoice always." Why is it so important to rejoice even when circumstances are terribly hard?*

---

8. *Why do you think it's so important to God that you come to Him in prayer and petition? Why doesn't He just supply what you need without asking?*

---

9. *In verse 8, Paul describes the kinds of things we should think about. What is helpful about his advice? Why is it likely to lead to peace?*

---

10. *What "secret" had Paul learned that enabled him to be content in every situation?*

11. *Take two minutes of silence to reread the passage, looking for a sentence, phrase, or even one word that stands out as something Jesus may want you to focus on in your life. If you're meeting with a group, the leader will keep track of time. At the end of two minutes, you may share with the group the word or phrase that came to you in the silence.*

12. *Read the passage aloud again. Take another two minutes of silence, prayerfully considering what response God might want you to make to what you have read in His Word. If you're meeting with a group, the leader will again keep track of time. At the end of two minutes, you may share with the group what came to you in the silence if you wish.*

13. *If you're meeting with a group, how can the members pray for you? If you're using this study on your own, what would you like to say to God right now?*

_____

_____

_____

_____

_____

LIVE IT

This week's daily Scripture readings focus on cultivating a life of peace that is found only in trusting God and relying on His strength. Read each passage slowly, pausing to think about what is being said. Rather than approaching this as an assignment to complete, think of it as an opportunity to meet with a Person. Use any of the questions that are helpful.

Day 1

Read Romans 15:13. What is the connection between hope and peace?

_____

_____

_____

_____

What is the connection between trust in God and peace?

How do you think it will affect other people if you overflow with hope? What will it take for you to reach this point of overflowing?

Tell the God of hope that you trust Him in today's circumstances. Ask Him to fill you with joy and peace.

Day 2

Read John 16:33. Jesus says that in the world, you will have trouble. What trouble do you have to deal with today?

How can you have peace despite that trouble?

_____

_____

_____

How has Jesus overcome the world?

_____

_____

_____

_____

Take your trouble to Jesus in prayer today and ask Him to overcome it, giving you peace in the midst of your trials.

Day 3

Read John 20:19–21. The phrase "Peace be with you" was the normal way of saying hello in the culture of that day. What additional meaning did the circumstances of this scene give to these words, which Jesus said right after His crucifixion and resurrection?

_____

_____

_____

Why do you think Jesus showed His disciples the nail wounds in His hands and the spear wound in His side? How do those contribute to your peace?

How does peace connect with Jesus' words, "As the Father has sent me, I am sending you"?

If you are a follower of Jesus, thank Him today for giving you His peace. Thank Him also for sending you with the message of peace.

Day 4

Read Proverbs 3:1–4. What is the connection between keeping God's commands and experiencing His peace and prosperity?

What is faithfulness? How does faithfulness contribute to peace?

_____

_____

_____

_____

What does it mean to "bind" love and faithfulness "around your neck"? What would that look like in your life?

_____

_____

_____

_____

Ask Jesus to help you heed His commands today and show you the pathway to finding a deeper sense of peace.

Day 5

Read Proverbs 3:13–18. What are some benefits of gaining wisdom and understanding?

_____

_____

_____

How much do you value wisdom? What is the evidence in your life?

_____

_____

_____

How can you cultivate wisdom? How do you think gaining wisdom is different from obtaining mere information?

_____

_____

_____

As you close this week's study, ask God to show you what it means to rely on His wisdom and understanding, rather than on your own, so you can discover how to truly "not be anxious about anything" (Philippians 4:6).

GOD'S PEACE
THROUGH
INHERITANCE
IN CHRIST

CONSIDER IT

The word *inheritance* most commonly means to receive something from a parent or ancestor after that person has died. People set up a will to let the courts know to whom they want to pass their assets and possessions once their life on earth has ended. In so doing, they typically designate individuals who are members of their family and thus rightful heirs to their estate. God does something similar when we accept Jesus and become a part of His family. He chooses to accept us and designates us as His rightful heirs. And His inheritance to those who believe in Him is eternal life. The more aware of this spiritual inheritance we are, the more at peace we will be in spite of what is going on around us. In this session, we will explore truths and qualities that foster this sense of peace.

1. *What is one thing (if any) that has been left to you as part of an inheritance? What are some things you would like to leave to your children or loved ones?*

_____

_____

_____

_____

2. *When you were a child, what did your parents do that let you know you were secure in their love? Or what did they do that left you feeling insecure?*

_____

_____

_____

EXPERIENCE IT

"Every time you affirm your trust in Me, you put a coin into My treasury. Thus you build up equity in preparation for days of trouble. I keep safely in My Heart all trust invested in Me, with interest compounded continuously. The more you trust Me, the more I empower you to do so.

"Practice trusting Me during quiet days, when nothing much seems to be happening. Then when storms come, your trust balance will be sufficient to see you through. *Store up for yourself treasure in heaven*, through placing your trust in Me. This practice will keep you in My Peace."

—FROM *JESUS CALLING*, JANUARY 10

3. *Why should you work on trusting Christ now, rather than waiting until difficult days come?*

4. *How can you practice trusting Jesus during the "quiet days"?*

"You are Mine for all time—and beyond time, into eternity. No power can deny you your inheritance in heaven. I want you to realize how utterly secure you are! Even if you falter as you journey through life, I will never let go of your hand.

"Knowing that your future is absolutely assured can free you to live abundantly today. I have prepared this day for you with the most tender concern and attention to detail. Instead of approaching the day as a blank page that you need to fill up, try living it in a responsive mode, being on the lookout for all that I am doing. This sounds easy, but it requires a deep level of trust, based on the knowledge that My way is perfect."

—From *Jesus Calling*, March 10

5. *If you're a Christian, how can you know that your inheritance in heaven is "utterly secure"?*

_____

_____

_____

6. *What can you do if you find that what is going on around you really does disrupt your peace? How can you fortify your faith?*

_____

_____

_____

Study It

Read aloud the following passage from Colossians 3:12–17, 23–25. Note how Paul describes the Colossian believers and how that knowledge should affect their actions toward one another. Also note what he says about how their spiritual inheritance in Christ should affect their sense of peace.

[12] Therefore, as God's chosen people, holy and dearly loved, clothe yourselves with compassion, kindness, humility, gentleness and patience. [13] Bear with each other and forgive one another if any of you has a grievance against someone. Forgive as the Lord forgave you. [14] And over all these virtues put on love, which binds them all together in perfect unity.

[15] Let the peace of Christ rule in your hearts, since as members of one body you were called to peace. And be thankful. [16] Let the message of Christ dwell among you richly as you teach and admonish one another with all wisdom through psalms, hymns, and songs from the Spirit, singing to God with gratitude in your hearts. [17] And whatever you do, whether in word or deed, do it all in the name of the Lord Jesus, giving thanks to God the Father through him. . . .

[23] Whatever you do, work at it with all your heart, as working for the Lord, not for human masters, [24] since you know that you will receive an inheritance from the Lord as a reward. It is the Lord Christ you are serving. [25] Anyone who does wrong will be repaid for their wrongs, and there is no favoritism.

7. *Paul begins this passage by stating that all his counsel is based on the bedrock reality that the Colossian believers are chosen, holy, and dearly loved. What does it mean to be chosen in this context?*

_____

_____

_____

_____

_____

_____

8. *What do traits such as compassion, kindness, humility, gentleness, and patience say to other people? How do these traits foster peace between people?*

_____

_____

_____

_____

9. *How does forgiveness foster peace within our hearts? How does thankfulness enhance peace?*

_____

_____

_____

_____

10. *What does Paul say is the reward for living a life ruled by the peace of Christ? According to Paul, how should this affect the way we view serving others in this world?*

_____

_____

_____

_____

11. *Take two minutes of silence to reread the passage, looking for a sentence, phrase, or even one word that stands out as something Jesus may want you to focus on in your life. If you're meeting with a group, the leader will keep track of time. At the end of two minutes, you may share with the group the word or phrase that came to you in the silence.*

12. *Read the passage aloud again. Take another two minutes of silence, prayerfully considering what response God might want you to make to what you have read in His Word. If you're meeting with a group, the leader will again keep track of time. At the end of two minutes, you may share with the group what came to you in the silence if you wish.*

13. *If you're meeting with a group, how can the members pray for you? If you're using this study on your own, what would you like to say to God right now?*

LIVE IT

This week's daily Scripture readings focus on how you can receive peace based on the assurance that God has an eternal inheritance for you. Read each passage slowly, pausing to think about what is being said. Rather than approaching this as an assignment to complete, think of it as an opportunity to meet with a Person. Use any of the questions that are helpful.

Day 1

Read Ephesians 1:3–6. When did God choose believers in Christ? How is this significant?

For what goal did God choose His children? How is it possible for Christians to be blameless in His sight?

When Paul refers to "adoption to sonship" (verse 5), it means we have the full legal rights of adult heirs (Paul is thinking here of Roman law). What do you suppose heirs of God possess? How does this matter to you?

_____

_____

_____

_____

Thank God today for giving you the opportunity to have a spiritual inheritance in Christ. If you have accepted His offer, ask Him to help you live a life consistent with being chosen.

Day 2

Read Ephesians 1:11–12. Paul writes that God "predestines," or determines beforehand, those whom He chooses to be in His family (see also Romans 8:29–30). How do you react to this idea that God, in His sovereignty, chooses certain individuals to be saved?

_____

_____

_____

If you have accepted Jesus as your Lord and Savior, what difference does it make that God chose you to be a recipient of His eternal inheritance? How should this affect the way you live?

_____

_____

_____

Paul says that God works out everything according to His will for His children. This means that your life of faith will bring glory to Jesus, even if you don't think you're doing anything remarkable. How does that assurance affect the way you see yourself? The way you see God?

_____

_____

_____

Look for an opportunity today to live for the praise of Jesus' glory in a practical way.

Day 3

Read 1 Peter 2:4–5. What does this passage say about Jesus?

_____

_____

_____

Peter writes that if you're a Christian, you are like one of the stones being built together into a spiritual house (or a temple of the Holy Spirit). How does that affect the way you see yourself? The way you live?

As a Christian, you have also been chosen to be part of a "holy priesthood." What does this mean? What are the practical implications of this for your life?

Pay attention to how you are being built together with other believers into something bigger than you as individuals. Praise Jesus for making this possible.

Day 4

Read 1 Peter 2:6. What does this verse say about a believer's foundation in Christ?

What does Peter mean when he says that the one who trusts in Christ "will never be put to shame"? How does this relate to a believer's inheritance in Christ?

_____

_____

_____

In what ways does this promise give believers peace to face whatever comes their way?

_____

_____

_____

Thank Jesus today for promising that you will never be put to shame as long as you trust in Him. Go through your day today with that confidence.

Day 5

Read 1 Peter 2:9–10. Peter repeats the idea of believers being a priesthood here—but now it's not just a holy priesthood but also a royal priesthood. What actions and character qualities are appropriate for members of a royal priesthood?

_____

_____

_____

What is the importance of these words being true not just for you as an individual but also for you as part of a group: a chosen people, a royal priesthood, and a holy nation?

In what sense are believers in Christ "God's special possession" (verse 9)? How is this important to you?

If you are a follower of Jesus, thank God today for choosing you to be part of something much bigger than yourself. Thank Him for making you a part of His family and for the inheritance that He has promised to you in Jesus. Allow this truth to sink into your heart and bring you peace.

GOD'S PEACE
THROUGH SPIRITUAL
DISCIPLINE

CONSIDER IT

Discipline is not a popular topic today. It feels like the opposite of freedom, which is one of our culture's highest values. The idea that discipline can free us from the tyranny of our negative inclinations seems foreign to us. After all, aren't all of our hearts' desires good by definition? Unfortunately, the answer is *no*. We are fallen, and left to ourselves our hearts will run off chasing all manner of unhelpful things. So, in this final week of study, we will see how God uses the hardship that inevitably comes into our lives to shape us into the people we were born to be. While hardship isn't pleasant, God can always use it for good.

1. *What comes to mind when you think of the word discipline? Explain.*

---

2. *How did your parents discipline you and your siblings when you were a child? How has that shaped the way you think about discipline as an adult?*

EXPERIENCE IT

"Refresh yourself in the Peace of My Presence. This Peace can be your portion at all times and in all circumstances. Learn to *hide in the secret of My Presence*, even as you carry out your duties in the world. I am both with you and within you. I go before you to open up the way, and I also walk alongside you. There could never be another companion as devoted as I am.

"Because I am your constant Companion, there should be a lightness to your step that is observable to others. Do not be weighed down with problems and unresolved issues, for I am your burden-bearer. In the world you have trials and distress, but don't let them get you down. *I have conquered the world and deprived it of power to harm you. In Me* you may have confident Peace."

—FROM *JESUS CALLING*, JANUARY 3

3. *What do you think it means to hide in the secret of Jesus' presence?*

_____

_____

_____

_____

4. *God promises in His Word to be every Christian's constant companion and shelter during the storm. Why do you think He doesn't just remove the hardships altogether?*

_____

_____

_____

_____

"Learn to live above your circumstances. This requires focused time with Me, the *One who overcame the world*. Trouble and distress are woven into the very fabric of this perishing world. Only My Life in you can empower you to face this endless flow of problems with *good cheer*.

"As you sit quietly in My Presence, I shine Peace into your troubled mind and heart. Little by little, you are freed from earthly shackles and lifted up above your circumstances. You gain My perspective on your life, enabling you to distinguish between what is important and what is not. Rest in My Presence, *receiving Joy that no one can take away from you*."

—FROM *JESUS CALLING*, MARCH 13

5. *How can the discipline of spending focused time with Christ each day enable you to live with thankfulness in spite of the problems you encounter?*

_____

_____

_____

6. *What tends to hinder you from spending time with Jesus every day? What things help you remember to regularly set aside this time?*

_____

_____

_____

STUDY IT

Read aloud the following passage from Hebrews 12:7–13. In these verses, the author draws on imagery that would have been familiar to the readers of his time: a loving father guiding and instructing his children. In that role, the father would have been *expected* to discipline his children to direct them back on the right path. Likewise, God the Father will sometimes lovingly discipline us—His beloved children—when we go astray. This discipline is not pleasant, but it does produce the type of change in our lives that brings spiritual growth and peace.

> [7] Endure hardship as discipline; God is treating you as his children. For what children are not disciplined by their father? [8] If you are not disciplined—and everyone undergoes discipline—then you are not legitimate, not true sons and daughters at all. [9] Moreover, we have all had human fathers who disciplined us and we respected them for it. How much more should we submit to the Father of spirits and live! [10] They disciplined us for a little while as they thought best; but God disciplines us for our good, in order that we may share in his holiness. [11] No discipline seems pleasant at the time, but painful. Later on, however, it produces a harvest of righteousness and peace for those who have been trained by it. [12] Therefore, strengthen your feeble arms and weak knees. [13] "Make level paths for your feet," so that the lame may not be disabled, but rather healed.

7. *The writer of Hebrews says that discipline produces "a harvest of righteousness and peace for those who have been trained by it" (verse 11). Are you surprised to think of painful circumstances as potentially leading to righteousness and peace? Explain your answer.*

_____

_____

_____

8. *Does it help to know that, if you're a child of God, some hardships can be discipline coming from your heavenly Father? Why or why not?*

_____

_____

_____

_____

9. *Have you experienced a growing peace resulting from a time of hardship? If so, share your experience to encourage the group.*

_____

_____

_____

_____

10. *The writer finishes by saying, "strengthen your feeble arms and weak knees" (verse 12). What does this mean in terms of how you should view hardships in your life?*

_____

_____

_____

_____

11. *Take two minutes of silence to reread the passage, looking for a sentence, phrase, or even one word that stands out as something Jesus may want you to focus on in your life. If you're meeting with a group, the leader will keep track of time. At the end of two minutes, you may share with the group the word or phrase that came to you in the silence.*

12. *Read the passage aloud again. Take another two minutes of silence, prayerfully considering what response God might want you to make to what you have read in His Word. If you're meeting with a group, the leader will again keep track of time. At the end of two minutes, you may share with the group what came to you in the silence if you wish.*

13. *If you're meeting with a group, how can the members pray for you? If you're using this study on your own, what would you like to say to God right now?*

LIVE IT

This week's daily Scripture readings focus on how spiritual discipline from your heavenly Father can help you develop peace in your life of faith. Read each passage slowly, pausing to think about what is being said. Rather than approaching this as an assignment to complete, think of it as an opportunity to meet with a Person. Use any of the questions that are helpful.

Day 1

Read Romans 5:3–5. What benefits can believers in Christ gain from suffering?

_____

_____

_____

_____

If this is true, why do you think so many Christians often do not benefit from suffering? What makes the difference for a person who gains perseverance, character, and hope from suffering as opposed to bitterness and despair?

_____

_____

_____

_____

Think about a time when you experienced suffering. Did you grow from it? Why do you think that was the case? How did your awareness of God's love make a difference?

Take a moment to thank God for pouring His love into your heart so you have what it takes to become a better person through your trials and struggles.

Day 2

Read 1 Peter 1:3–5. Peter speaks here about a "living hope," which means confident expectation. What can believers confidently expect because of the resurrection of Jesus Christ?

Peter writes of "an inheritance that can never perish, spoil or fade" (verse 4). How does having God's promise of such an inheritance as a believer help you have peace in the midst of difficult circumstances?

The apostle declares that, through faith, believers are shielded by God's power (see verse 5). What are you shielded from? What are you not shielded from? How does this affect your peace?

_____

_____

_____

_____

_____

If you have accepted Jesus as your Lord and Savior, praise God today for your living hope and guaranteed inheritance because of what He has done for you. Allow your heart to settle into an attitude of peace because of these promises.

Day 3

Read 1 Peter 1:6–9. Peter says that as a follower of Christ, you can greatly rejoice in your living hope and your inheritance, even though for a little while you may have to suffer grief in trials. How does your confident hope for the future affect the way you face trials now?

_____

_____

_____

_____

Like the apostle Paul, Peter talks about the value of trials for those who believe in Christ. What value does he discuss in verse 7? How important is this value to you? Why?

_____

_____

_____

Peter says that believers are filled with joy because they recognize they have received the salvation of their soul. As a Christian, does thinking about your salvation fill you with joy? Why or why not? How does that lead to peace?

_____

_____

_____

Tell God today about the abundant joy you feel because of your salvation—a joy that you have even in the midst of trials.

Day 4

Read James 1:2–5. James, like Paul, says that the testing of your faith produces perseverance (see verse 3). What is perseverance? Why is it valuable?

_____

_____

_____

What do you make of the fact that all these New Testament writers emphasize the joy believers in Christ can have in the midst of suffering? Why do you suppose this is a consistent biblical theme?

_____

_____

_____

James encourages believers to ask God if they need wisdom for dealing with trials (see verse 5). Is there some situation in your life for which you need wisdom? If so, how does James give you peace about this?

_____

_____

_____

If you are a follower of Christ, ask Him for wisdom in dealing with the circumstances of your life. Then release those circumstances to Him, knowing that His wisdom will be given to you.

Day 5

Read Romans 8:16–25. What reason for willingly sharing in Jesus' sufferings does Paul provide in verse 17? How do you respond?

_____

_____

What reason for having peace in the midst of suffering does Paul provide to believers in verse 18? How does this verse affect you?

As a believer, do you have the hope Paul discusses in verses 23–25? If so, how does this hope impact you in the here-and-now when problems arise? How much of it do you tend to regard as reserved for "way out in the future?" How can you strike a better balance?

Thank God today for the glory ahead of you as a follower of Christ: the redemption of your body. Pray about this until you can feel the hope and longing for what God has promised to do.

LEADER'S NOTES

Thank you for your willingness to lead a group through this *Jesus Calling* study. The rewards of leading are different from the rewards of participating, and we hope you find your own walk with Jesus deepened by this experience. In many ways, your group meeting will be structured like other Bible studies in which you've participated. You'll want to open in prayer, for example, and ask people to silence their phones. These leader's notes will focus on elements of the study that may be new to you.

CONSIDER IT

This first portion of the study functions as an icebreaker. It gets the group members thinking about the topic at hand by asking them to share things from their own experience. Some people may be tempted to tell a long story in response to one of these questions, but the goal is to keep the answers brief. Ideally, you want everyone in the group to have a chance to answer the *Consider It* questions, so you may want to say up front that everyone needs to limit his or her answer to one minute.

With the rest of the study, it is generally not a good idea to go around the circle and have everyone answer every question—a free-flowing discussion is more desirable. But with the *Consider It* questions, you can go around the circle. Encourage shy people to share, but don't force them. Tell the group they should feel free to pass if they prefer not to answer a question.

EXPERIENCE IT

This is the group's chance to talk about excerpts from the *Jesus Calling* devotional. You will need to monitor this discussion closely so that you have enough time for the actual study of God's Word that follows. If the group has a long and rich discussion on one of the devotional excerpts, you may choose to skip the other one and move on to the Bible study. Don't feel obliged to cover every *Experience It* question if the conversation is fruitful. On the other hand, do move on if the group gets off on a tangent.

STUDY IT

Try to do the *Study It* exercise in session 1 on your own before the group meets the first time so you can coach people on what to expect. Note that this section may be a little different from Bible studies your group has done in the past. The group will talk about the Bible passage as usual, but then there will be several minutes of silence so individuals can pray about what God might want to say to them personally through the reading. It will be up to you to keep track of the time and call people back to the discussion when the time is up. (There are some good timer apps that play a gentle chime or other pleasant sound instead of a disruptive noise.) If the group members aren't used to being silent in a group, brief them on what to expect.

Don't be afraid to let people sit in silence. Two minutes of quiet may seem like a long time at first, but it will help to train group members to sit in silence with God when they are alone. They can remain where they are in the circle, or if you have space, you can let them go off by themselves to other rooms at your instruction. If your group meets in a home, ask the host before the meeting which rooms are available for use. Some people will be more comfortable in the quiet if they have a bit of space from others.

When the group reconvenes after the time of silence, invite them to share what they experienced. There are several questions provided in this study guide that you can ask. Note that it's not necessary to cover every question if the group has a good discussion going. It's also not necessary to go around the circle and make everyone share.

Don't be concerned if the group members are reserved and slow to share after the exercise. People are often quiet when they are pulling together their ideas, and the exercise will have been a new experience for many of them. Just ask a question and let it hang in the air until someone speaks up. You can then say, "Thank you. What about others? What came to you when you sat with the passage?"

Some people may say they found it hard to quiet their minds enough to focus on the passage for those few minutes. Tell them this is okay. They are practicing a skill, and sometimes skills take time to learn. If they learn to sit quietly with God's Word in a group, they will become much more comfortable sitting with the Word on their own. Remind them that spending time in the Bible each day is one of the most valuable things they can do as believers in Christ.

PREPARATION

It's not necessary for group members to prepare anything for the study ahead of time. However, at the end of each study are five days' worth of suggestions for spending time in God's Word during the next week. These daily times are optional but valuable, so encourage the group to do them. Also, invite them to bring their questions and insights to the group at your next meeting, especially if they had a breakthrough moment or if they didn't understand something.

As the leader, there are a few things you should do to prepare for each meeting:

- *Read through the session.* This will help you become familiar with the content and know how to structure the discussion times.

- *Spend five to ten minutes doing the* Study It *questions on your own.* When the group meets, you'll be watching the clock, so you'll probably have a more fulfilling time with the passage if you do the exercise ahead of time. You can then spend time in the passage again with the group. This way, you'll be sure to have the key verses for that session deeply in your mind.

- *Pray for your group.* Pray especially that God will guide them into a deeper understanding of how they can learn to continually dwell in His peace.

- *Bring extra supplies to your meeting.* Group members should bring their own pens for writing notes on the Bible reflection, but it is a good idea to have extras available for those who forget. You may also want to bring paper and Bibles for those who may have neglected to bring their study guides to the meeting.

Below you will find suggested answers for some of the study questions. Note that in many cases there is no one right answer, especially when the group members are sharing their personal experiences.

Session 1: God's Peace through Faith in Christ

1. *An example would include having a childhood that was peaceful to a degree—they had food, clothing, and shelter, as well as stable schooling—but* *they lived in a household that was rocked by constant conflict or upheaval. Such an experience is bound to color their experience of peace today.*

2. *Some of the group members may feel their lives are fairly peaceful even though they are busy, while others might be troubled by a lack of peace even though their circumstances are essentially stable. A non-peaceful childhood and a lack of the peace that Jesus offers can easily affect people's perceptions.*

3. *Jesus gave up His life and rose again to make it possible for us to be at peace with God and thus with ourselves. Our sinful rebellion and stubborn efforts to live on our own erected a barrier between us and God, but Jesus died to reconcile us with God.*

4. *We know that adverse circumstances are a normal part of life, but they still take many of us by surprise because we think a good God would want us to feel good. It's important for believers in Christ to recognize that adversity is normal and that God is taking care of us in the midst of those adverse circumstances. He has promised to always be with us in both the good times and the bad.*

5. *The realization that Jesus died a criminal's death for us should move us to profound gratitude. If we have accepted this gift, it should also motivate us to trust in the One who went to such lengths to bring us peace. We can go through our days overjoyed, even if circumstances are difficult, because the most important thing we need—peace with our heavenly Father—has been provided for us. If ever we doubt that we matter to Jesus, we can think of what He went through for us and be reassured.*

6. *Answers will vary, but sitting quietly in Jesus' presence is an important practice that needs to become our habit. Just doing this for ten minutes a day is a great start. We will hear a lot of internal noise at first, but as we gently return our attention to Jesus, the noise will clear away and we will gradually become aware of His peace. Rather than emptying our minds, as some* *religions prescribe, we fill them with thoughts of His loving sacrifice on our behalf.*

7. *Inner peace minus peace with God is self-deception. To feel at peace when we are not placing our eternal destiny in God's hands means we are abiding in a false sense of security. We need to make sure our relationship with God is based on following His commands and submitting to Him to deal with the sin in our hearts. Only when our consciences are legitimately clear can we really be at peace.*

8. *Jesus' death and resurrection makes peace with God possible. God has extended the gift of salvation to us, but we need to reach out and accept the gift. Faith is that "reaching out." Faith, or trust in Jesus, is the way we accept what God has offered to us.*

9. *Paul uses many terms to get at the same basic idea. When we reconcile with God, it means the wall of hostility has been torn down and we are now God's friends, saved from the punishment of sin. Even more, we are God's beloved children. Friendship with God is the bedrock of our peace with God.*

10. *Many people, even Christians, don't experience peace with God as a day-to-day reality. They go about their lives feeling insecure and unsure of how God views them. But it doesn't have to be that way. (Be sure to pray with any group members who don't have this peace with God—pray that they will put their faith in Jesus and receive the peace He offers.)*

11. *Answers will vary. It's fine for this process to be unfamiliar to the group at first. Be sure to watch the time.*

12. *Answers will vary. Note that some people may find the silence intimidating at first. Their anxiety might tempt them to fill the air with noise, but it will be helpful for these group members to just take a quiet moment before God. Let them express their discomfort once you're all gathered* *together again, but make sure it is balanced by those who found the silence strengthening. Helping people become comfortable with this "holy quiet" will serve their private daily times with God in wonderful ways.*

13. *Take as much time as you can to pray for each other. You might have someone write down the prayer requests so you can keep track of answered prayers.*

Session 2: God's Peace through Obedience to Christ

1. *Answers will vary. Consider giving an answer of your own that is about a minute long and moderately personal to model what you'd like the group to do. You don't want members to share overly long stories about their childhood—you just want to get them thinking about how they responded to the idea of obedience in their upbringing.*

2. *Again, urge the group to be brief with their answers and not divulge anything too personal.*

3. *For many believers in Christ, that "true Center" is a felt reality. Others need to operate more by faith in Someone they don't necessarily feel. Whether we consistently feel Jesus' Presence or not, we each need to practice dialing down the external voices that clamor for our attention and take time for solitude each day to focus our hearts and minds on Him.*

4. *Even the closest human relationships are subject to changes beyond our control. Family members move away, friends find themselves with less time to devote to the relationship, and children tend to drain away the time we can devote to friendships. Only God is completely reliable, and Scripture promises that He is "the same yesterday and today and forever" (Hebrews 13:8). Lasting peace can only be found in Him.*

5. *We all make plans for the day ahead of us, but the point is not to get so caught up in scheduling it that we miss out on the opportunities God places* *in our path. The subtle voices in our minds often say, "My agenda is what's important," or, "If I'm not doing this, it means I'm a failure." Instead, we need to be in tune with Jesus, trust in Him for direction, and allow Him to guide and direct our steps each day.*

6. *As the leader, you don't need to be the first to answer this, but when others have had a chance to speak, add your experience. Be sure to stress that walking with Jesus is always an adventure. While the uncertainty this brings may cause some apprehension (especially if we like lots of control!), we can be assured that when we are obedient to Christ and walking on His path as directed in Scripture and through the daily guidance of the Holy Spirit, God's peace will go with us.*

7. *To love Jesus is to be convinced that He is the King of the universe, the One who knows how things ought to go, and the One with the wisdom and right to guide us. We show we love Him when we demonstrate He is sovereign over our lives. It simply doesn't make sense to say in our hearts, "I know that Jesus deserves to be obeyed, but I'm not going to obey Him."*

8. *Jesus is no longer bodily with us on earth; He now speaks through the Holy Spirit, who lives within each of His followers. The Spirit is called the Advocate because He comes alongside us and guides us as a caring lawyer would guide us through a maze of legal proceedings. The Spirit also reminds us of the things that Jesus says in the Bible.*

9. *If we love Jesus, we show that love by choosing to obey Him—and we have the Holy Spirit guiding us in how best to obey Him for our good. This secure guidance lets us experience His peace. Obedience thus leads ultimately to experiencing the peace of Christ.*

10. *Jesus is referring here to the spiritual inheritance that He is leaving His followers. Unlike the world, He is not leaving them with material possessions, but with "the peace of God, which transcends all understanding" (Philippians*

4:7). Unlike the things of the world, which are temporary and fleeting in nature, this gift from Christ will never pass away.

11. *Answers will vary.*

12. *Answers will vary.*

13. *Responses will vary.*

Session 3: God's Peace through the Work of the Holy Spirit

1. *Some common misunderstandings about the Holy Spirit include: (1) He is only present at certain times; (2) He only works through "miraculous" events; (3) He always acts spontaneously; and (4) He will take over our will. The truth about the Holy Spirit is that: (1) He is always with us; (2) He guides us even in the mundane things of life; (3) He directs us more on a day-by-day basis as we grow in Christ rather than through "spontaneous" events; and (4) He leads us and guides us, but he will never force us to do something against our will.*

2. *The Bible passage being studied today will contrast the peace we get from setting our minds on the things of the Spirit versus the lack of peace from setting our minds on the things of the flesh. It will be interesting to see how the war between flesh and Spirit might be at work in the events that group members mention. Be sure not to call out those who had a lack of peace today—they are not inferior to those who had peace. We are all in process, and rough days are part of that process.*

3. *Seeking understanding for the purpose of controlling our circumstances is not a good way to pursue peace because life gives us an endless series of problems to solve. If we require mastery over every problem in order to have peace, we will quickly find ourselves overwhelmed. Instead, we need to trust that the Holy Spirit is working in* *our lives and that He will give us the understanding we need to move to the next step in our walk with God.*

4. *In John 14:27, Jesus said to His disciples, "Peace I leave with you; my peace I give you. I do not give to you as the world gives. Do not let your hearts be troubled and do not be afraid." Jesus left His peace to us, His followers, and the Holy Spirit will make us aware of that peace by showing us the way to walk in step with God's will. As we choose to follow God each day, seeking His peace and His strength above the things of this world, we begin to experience the peace that only He can provide.*

5. *Keeping our minds focused on God comes with practice. When we first establish a daily time with Him—praying and reading His Word—it can be difficult to be still in His presence. Some practical tips for combating this problem include repeating a line of Scripture, such as "Be still, and know that I am God" (Psalm 46:10), or "The mind governed by the Spirit is life and peace" (Romans 8:6). If our mind wanders, we can gently bring it back to the biblical passage we are reflecting on. The key is to keep returning our thoughts to the God who loves us, and to the truths of His Word, so we can learn to discern how the Holy Spirit is leading us throughout our day.*

6. *Answers will vary, but this is a skill that requires practice and persistence. Though our thoughts will wander in the beginning, over time we will find it easier to turn what enters our mind over to Jesus. The Holy Spirit provides the ability to do what we can't do on our own.*

7. *Examples include money, possessions, other people's approval, status, power, or even eternal youthfulness. It's normal to long for intimacy and purpose—to want to be loved and needed. However, when we pursue these desires apart from the Lord, they can become grasping demands that are never satisfied. Focusing on people or things can never make us feel permanently and unconditionally loved or fulfilled.*

8. *The Holy Spirit desires to make us holy. He wants to connect us with Jesus so that we experience authentic intimacy and lasting purpose. The Spirit desires for all people to know and love Christ. He wants the people of God to be shining lights that point others toward Jesus.*

9. *The mind that is set on the flesh's desires is stuck in a perpetual hunger for things that can never satisfy it. It is driven toward desires that actually only rob us of peace. But the Holy Spirit helps us as believers hunger for things that will truly satisfy and give us peace, such as genuine intimacy with Jesus.*

10. *If we belong to Christ, the knowledge that we reside in the realm of the Spirit will give us peace. We know that even though our physical bodies are gradually dying, the Spirit is continually giving us spiritual life. And we look forward to the promise of resurrection from the dead—when we will be alive in a transformed body eternally. Nothing that happens to us as believers in this life can ultimately harm us, because we are promised eternal life with Jesus in heaven.*

11. *Answers will vary.*

12. *Answers will vary.*

13. *Responses will vary.*

Session 4: God's Peace in the Midst of Suffering

1. *Answers will vary, but it's important to note that our reflexive response to suffering is often something we learn as children. Maybe our parents coped with hard times by getting angry or depressed, by remaining in denial, or by withdrawing. Or maybe they tackled problems head on. Regardless of how they coped, we need to remember that when the storms of life come, Jesus calls us to lean into Him, trust Him with the answer, and choose to dwell in His peace.*

2. *We have a fundamental need to know why certain things are happening to us, and when those answers are not forthcoming, it causes us to question God and even doubt His concern for us. Some of the greatest men and women in the Bible felt the absence of God during times of crisis, including the prophet Isaiah, who once declared, "You have hidden your face from us and have given us over to our sins" (Isaiah 64:7). Perhaps this is why the Bible is filled with so many promises of God's continual love and care. As God said to Isaiah, "When you pass through the waters, I will be with you; and when you pass through the rivers, they will not sweep over you" (Isaiah 43:2).*

3. *Answers will vary. This can be difficult for any follower of Christ. Once again, it comes down to our basic trust that God is loving and has our best interests in mind—that He is "the Mighty Warrior who saves" (Zephaniah 3:17). Cultivating a daily practice of spending time in Jesus' presence can help build our faith and trust that He will provide for us in life's small things. This in turn prepares us to trust Him when the larger crises arrive. The key is to be intentional about this habit so we can learn to recognize the small blessings He provides each day to show that He cares.*

4. *What we choose to do during times of trial can either magnify God's glory in others' eyes or diminish it. While we can't lessen His glory in an absolute sense—He is who He is—we can obscure what others perceive about His glory by the way we live. Persevering during times of struggle not only deepens our own trust in Him, but it serves as a powerful example of faith for those who are watching how we react.*

5. *Answers will vary. On good days, peace may come more naturally. But during times of suffering, the contrast between the pain and Jesus' peace is vivid. This is one of the ways God uses the inevitable suffering that we as Christians experience as we go through life. We learn to recognize and embrace Jesus' peace.*

6. *"Spiritual training" is something we as believers do over time—for months and years. We sit with Jesus each day and get into the habit of clothing ourselves with His peace. We connect with Him throughout our day, asking for His peace as anxious situations arise. Then, when times of darkness come, we find it much easier to practice peace that overcomes the darkness.*

7. *Satan accuses Job of respecting God and shunning evil only because the Lord has bought his allegiance with material blessings. At stake is the question of whether Job loves God for Himself or loves Him only because of the gifts He has provided. If people love God only for His gifts, it does not represent true love for their Creator.*

8. *God knows that Job worships Him for Himself, and He shows His confidence by allowing Satan to prove Him right. He honors Job—though in our minds it's an excruciating way to honor someone! This story reveals that one reason God might allow suffering is to prove our faith. Job's example is an extreme case, but it opens up the possibility that God is displaying our faith when He allows something bad to happen to us.*

9. *Job's acts of shaving his head and tearing his clothes are signs of deep grief. His words express anguish but also the belief that God has a right to allow what He has allowed. Job continues to believe God is good, so he praises God's name. Job knows nothing about the conversation between God and Satan. He doesn't know the angels are looking on to see what he does. But he does know that God is King and thus has a right, as the Giver of all things, to take away His gifts.*

10. *Job's anguish is acute, which makes sense given the tragedies he has recently endured. But his attitude is such that while he is not exactly at peace, he's on the right road to restored peace because he insists on trusting the Lord. As the story of Job progresses, more bad things happen to him, and he does complain bitterly to God (see Job 10:1–8). But when he experiences God at the end of the story, later in his life, he makes his way back to peace (see Job 42:2–6).*

11. *Answers will vary.*

12. *Answers will vary.*

13. *Responses will vary.*

Session 5: God's Peace among Believers in Christ

1. *Answers will vary. This question isn't so much about what we actually do when disagreements arise as it is about what we are tempted to do when conflict comes our way. Encourage everyone in the group to be honest about their natural inclinations.*

2. *Answers will vary. As we will explore in this session, God calls us as Christians to live at peace with our fellow believers—to love one another as He loves us (see John 13:34)—so the ultimate goal is to be moving toward unity and reconciliation in the body of Christ.*

3. *Being still before Jesus—relaxing in His presence—allows us as believers to slow the anxious thoughts that dart around in our minds and refocus on Him. Note that the goal isn't to "empty our minds" (as is practiced in Buddhism) but to fill our minds with an awareness of Jesus' Presence and receive the guidance of His Spirit.*

4. *We may think nothing we can do will affect Jesus. But that's not true. The Bible indicates that Jesus' followers add to His overflowing joy when they worship Him and rest in His Presence, and that they add to His pain when they tie themselves up in anxious knots and refuse to trust Him. Hopefully this thought will help motivate us to lay our anxieties at His feet and take the time to cultivate trust in Him.*

5. *Seeking the approval of others is a widespread problem in our society— even among believers in Christ. When our goal is always to please others (offering them the "dry crumbs" that we think will please them), it reduces* our witness for Christ (the "living water" of the Holy Spirit). We need to be real with each other, both in our strengths and our weakness, and focus on Jesus' opinion of us rather than the opinions of others.

6. There are many ways to stay in touch with Jesus even during your busiest times when you are tempted to just react to what others say. One way is to pause before you speak or act and silently ask Jesus to guide your response. James notes the importance of doing this when he writes, "My dear brothers and sisters, take note of this: Everyone should be quick to listen, slow to speak and slow to become angry, because human anger does not produce the righteousness that God desires" (James 1:19–20).

7. Paul says that we were foreigners and strangers as far as God was concerned. We were separate from Christ and excluded from citizenship with God's people, without hope and without God or His promises. This was a very serious problem.

8. It's very important for believers in Christ to see themselves as part of a family, regardless of the language they speak or the customs they practice. In our world, ethnicity tends to divide people—but it shouldn't be that way. Just as Jesus wants us to trust Him and not tie ourselves up in anxious knots, so He also wants us to have peace with each other.

9. The dividing wall may be harm done by that other person that hasn't been forgiven, or it might be two different ways of looking at life. Whatever it is, give group members a moment of silence to think about those relationships that have caused them a lack of peace and what circumstances have come between them.

10. It is so important to Jesus that we have peace in our relationships. He died to make it possible! He wants all who belong to Him to see each other as members of the same family. Encourage the group members to commit to contact someone they've been avoiding. Or, if the relationship is not reconcilable, encourage them to at least let go of their inner demand for fairness and forgive the other person.

11. *Answers will vary.*

12. *Answers will vary.*

13. *Responses will vary.*

Session 6: God's Peace through the Practice of Prayer

1. *Some examples might include being financially secure, having the right friends and business associates, getting lots of likes on Facebook, driving a nice car, having a nice house, having your kids in the right schools . . . the list is endless.*

2. *Let the group members give an honest assessment of what they tend to do to find peace in a chaotic day and whether they feel this actually works most of the time. During the study, the group will be looking at Paul's counsel in Philippians 4:4–13 about the secret of being content in any and every situation, and it will be interesting for members to reflect back on this question in light of that advice.*

3. *Self-sufficiency is a trap first of all because it is an illusion. We may think we can manage life on our own, but we can never guarantee a supply of the things that make life worth living—they all come from God. Self-sufficiency is also a trap because it causes us to stray from God, who is the source of our very life. We go down a path that leads to eternal separation from God.*

4. *Ideally we are all aware of our neediness, but in reality some of us aren't as aware of it. We drive like a tank through life, confident in ourselves and our abilities. Others of us feel a deep sense of neediness, but we never get a warm feeling of Jesus' sufficiency or trustworthiness. In that case, we need to learn to live by faith rather than by feelings.*

5. *This is a good chance to get to know what "sea of problems" your group members are facing and how they see God working in their lives in the midst of those trials. Let people share, but be sure to watch the clock so that no one goes on and on about their problems and hinders the rest of the study. It may be appropriate in some cases to pause for a brief prayer for those who have shared particular struggles.*

6. *Throughout the Bible, we are advised to call on God in the midst of trouble (see, for example, Psalm 34:17; Psalm 50:15; Jeremiah 33:3; and Isaiah 43:2). The most important thing is for us to stay close to Jesus and trust in Him, rather than fixating on the problems. This is especially true if the problems are in the future. Worrying doesn't accomplish anything useful. If we get overwhelmed, we can cry out, "Help me, Jesus!"*

7. *We can always rejoice because we know that nothing can ultimately harm us. This attitude of rejoicing will make our faith attractive to others, and they will want to know how we are able to be so joyful. When they ask, our answer as Christians can be, "The worst that could happen to me is death, and even then I will be with Jesus."*

8. *God wants us to be aware of our dependence on Him, and He also wants us to form the quality of humility (having to ask for things teaches us humility). Furthermore, asking and giving are fundamental parts of a loving relationship. God wants us to love Him enough to ask Him for things and to be grateful when He responds.*

9. *Paul doesn't want us to pretend the bad and ugly things don't exist. Yet he wants us to fill our minds with good and praiseworthy things, because where our minds go, our bodies and emotions will follow. Many of us are hardwired to attend to negative things as a protective strategy, so we don't need to be told to pay attention to the dangerous and unpleasant things. We do that naturally. What doesn't come naturally is balancing that with attending to the good things.*

10. *It's hard to understand how a person could have peace while sitting in a jail cell waiting to find out whether he's going to be executed. Yet Paul had this peace because he had learned the secret of trusting in God for provision day by day and rejoicing in the fact that God had saved him eternally. Paul could do "all this" in his ministry because God gave him the strength each day.*

11. *Answers will vary.*

12. *Answers will vary.*

13. *Responses will vary.*

Session 7: God's Peace through Inheritance in Christ

1. *Have some fun with this question and let group members reminisce for a few minutes about what they have inherited from a loved one or hope to pass along to future descendants. Be sure to ask why those objects they received or want to give are especially meaningful to them.*

2. *This is a fairly personal question, but you have been together long enough that group members should be able to be honest about their insecurity if that was the reality for them when they were growing up. It's a lot easier to believe God has chosen us as His children if we come from a background that made us feel chosen and loved as children. But even if we don't come from that kind of environment, God can rewrite our stories and rewire our minds with the truth that He is a Father who chooses us and never lets us go.*

3. *We are creatures of habit, and even the way we think can become habitual. So, if we willfully remind ourselves to trust Christ day by day, our minds will be established in this habit by the time we hit a day when trust is hard. Likewise, if we rely on ourselves each day, that will be our first inclination even on days when we would like to respond differently.*

4. *Answers will vary. We can take a few moments to pray, "I trust You, Jesus," throughout the day. Because we know Christ, we can embrace each thing that happens with conscious confidence that Jesus is giving us what is good. We can thank Him for what comes. We can keep turning our thoughts to Him. All of these patterns that we establish during the quiet times will build a habit of prayer and trust that we as Christians can rely on during the not-so-quiet times.*

5. *In 2 Corinthians 4:18, Paul tells believers to fix their eyes "not on what is seen, but on what is unseen, since what is seen is temporary, but what is unseen is eternal." In this world we will experience crises that shake us to our core, but our ability to trust in God in the midst of them—and even thank Him for the comfort He provides—will reveal a great deal as to whether our innermost being is truly grounded in eternity. This again involves trusting and noticing God's provision in life's "little things" so that when catastrophe comes, we have an established faith in Him.*

6. *Try taking a break several times a day to refocus your thoughts and pray, "Jesus, give me Your peace." And take daily time for a longer period of prayer. You need to immerse yourself in the presence of Jesus, and building these habits will be a great help.*

7. *Being chosen simply means that a person belongs to Jesus. The person doesn't find Jesus; rather, Jesus goes out in search of that lost person and brings him or her to Himself. Christ expresses this truth in the parable of the lost sheep: "If a man owns a hundred sheep, and one of them wanders away, will he not leave the ninety-nine on the hills and go to look for the one that wandered off? And if he finds it, truly I tell you, he is happier about that one sheep than about the ninety-nine that did not wander off. In the same way your Father in heaven is not willing that any of these little ones should perish" (Matthew 18:12–14). It's important for those of us who are Christians to reflect on this truth often so that our peace is rooted in the certainty that we belong to Someone who chose us, sought us, and dearly loves us.*

125

8. *Compassion, kindness, humility, gentleness, and patience are the antidote to the kind of anger that disrupts peace between people and within ourselves. These traits communicate to others that we understand them, feel for them, care about what they're going through, and value them as individuals. It's much harder to be at odds with someone when we have compassionately put ourselves in his or her shoes.*

9. *Forgiveness fosters peace within our hearts because it removes the weight of anger and allows us to "live lighter." It tears down the barriers we have set up against others, bringing inner rest. Likewise, thankfulness frees us from self-pity. It helps us focus on the good aspects of our lives while opening our eyes to the blessings of God. To realize the breadth and depth of God's mercy enables us to extend mercy to others—which frees us from unnecessary stress and anxiety.*

10. *Paul says that the reward for living a life ruled by the peace of Christ is the spiritual inheritance of eternal life with Jesus. In all we do, we should view ourselves as working for Christ rather than other people. This shift in our mindset will impact not only the work we do for God's kingdom but also how we feel about serving others.*

11. *Answers will vary.*

12. *Answers will vary.*

13. *Responses will vary.*

Session 8: God's Peace through Spiritual Discipline

1. *It's likely that at least some of your group members will have a negative reaction to discipline and view it solely in terms of punishment. Others might see discipline as a necessary means to achieve their goals, such as when they follow a weight-loss program or fitness regimen. Take a few minutes to discuss* these "first impressions" of discipline before diving in a bit deeper with the next question.

2. *Answers will vary. Some group members may have been disciplined harshly by their parents in anger. This can persuade a child to grow up to be a similarly harsh, angry person, or to resist discipline altogether, which can lead to resentment toward God if it is suggested that He disciplines His children. On the other hand, some group members may have grown up without discipline and now struggle as adults to discipline themselves. Still others may have had firm but loving parents who modeled the kind of "productive discipline" that God offers.*

3. *This is a reference to Psalm 31:20, where David writes, "In the shelter of your presence you hide them from all human intrigues; you keep them safe in your dwelling from accusing tongues." Jesus' presence is like a secret shelter where God's people can be safe from the harms of the world. We might be attacked verbally or even physically, but spiritually we are completely safe.*

4. *God often allows us to go through hardships so we will learn to depend on Him alone. When times are good and the skies are clear, it is easy to lose our focus on God and fail to see Him as our provider. However, when the storm clouds appear, we are quickly reminded that God is in control of everything in life—and only He can calm the raging winds and stormy seas. Hardships can serve as a form of spiritual discipline that will take us to the next level in learning to trust in the Lord.*

5. *To build the good habit of spending time in God's Word and in His presence helps us get His perspective on how to face our problems. This focused time with Jesus on a daily basis is crucial for our spiritual growth; the transformation doesn't happen all at once but little by little. Ultimately we learn to rely on His strength, turn to Him first when problems arise, trust Him for the outcome, and rest in the peace that only He provides.*

6. *Encourage people to share their challenges honestly. Mothers with small children and those who work long hours will obviously wonder where they will find the time to do this, but even carving out ten minutes a day for stillness with Jesus will make a difference in their lives. Ask those who have had success in building this quiet time into their routine to share what they found to be effective in keeping it each day (for example, setting an alarm on their phone to remind them, or making this the first thing they do each day, or carving out a set time in their work schedule to meet with God).*

7. *In many ways spiritual discipline produces results that resemble what happens when we join an exercise program. At first it is painful, and we wonder if the effort is really worth it. But as we stick to the program, we begin to see powerful changes in our lives in the form of more energy, better health, and a more positive outlook on life. As we stick with our spiritual "training," we begin to see good results in our lives in the form of righteousness and peace.*

8. *Some group members may find it helpful to think of their trials this way, because it gives meaning to the seemingly random difficulties that befall Christians through no fault of our own. Others may find it unhelpful, because they can't imagine a loving Father allowing—let alone using—the tragedies that strike them. In this it is helpful to know that when the writer to the Hebrews spoke of hardship as discipline, he had in mind the persecution his readers were suffering because of their faith. He wasn't thinking about unexplainable tragedies like a child's leukemia or a loved one's fatal car accident at the hands of a drunk driver.*

9. *Not everyone will have had this experience. It's often hard to draw a straight line from a time of suffering to a time of growth in our character. If you as leader have had a time of hardship, you may want to share what you see as the fruit of that time.*

10. *The idea is to think of all hardship as training rather than torture. Training has meaning and is a force for good. Torture has no meaning; it is* *wholly harmful, and it doesn't make us stronger. The important thing is that we get to choose whether we receive hardship as training or torture. We get to decide whether we use it to strengthen our "feeble arms."*

11. *Answers will vary.*

12. *Answers will vary.*

13. *Responses will vary.*

Also Available in the
Jesus Calling® Bible Study Series

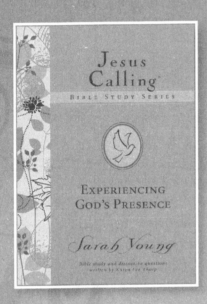

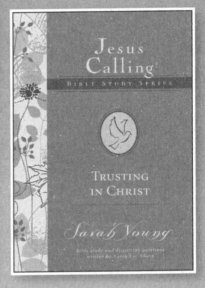

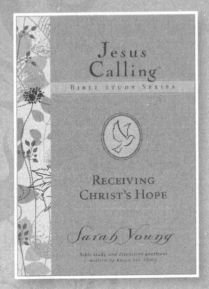

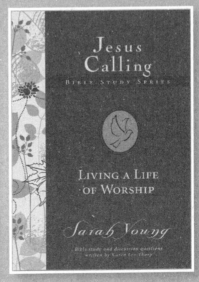

Also Available in the
Jesus Calling® Bible Study Series

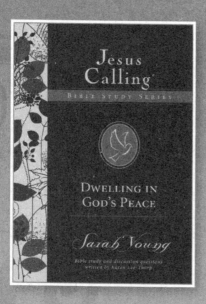

Jesus Calling®
BIBLE STUDY SERIES

DWELLING IN
GOD'S PEACE

Sarah Young

Bible study and discussion questions
written by Karen Lee-Thorp

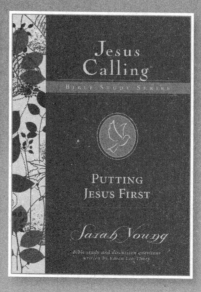

Jesus Calling®
BIBLE STUDY SERIES

PUTTING
JESUS FIRST

Sarah Young

Bible study and discussion questions
written by Karen Lee-Thorp

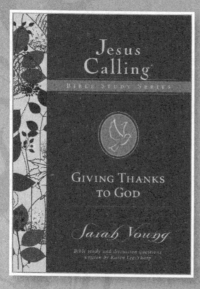

Jesus Calling®
BIBLE STUDY SERIES

GIVING THANKS
TO GOD

Sarah Young

Bible study and discussion questions
written by Karen Lee-Thorp

Jesus Calling®
BIBLE STUDY SERIES

LIVING WITH
GOD'S COURAGE

Sarah Young

Bible study and discussion questions
written by Karen Lee-Thorp

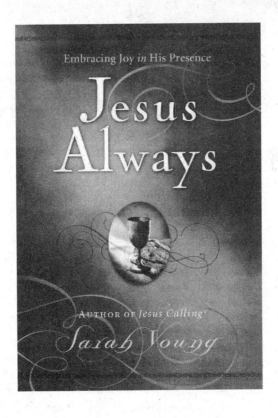

If you liked reading this book, you may enjoy these other titles by *Sarah Young*

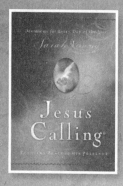

Jesus Calling®
Hardcover

Jesus Calling® 10th Anniversary Edition
Bonded Leather

Peace in His Presence:
Favorite Quotations from Jesus Calling®
Padded Hardcover

Jesus Calling® for Kids
Hardcover

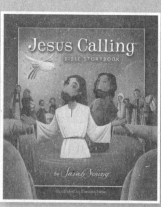

Jesus Calling® Bible Storybook
Hardcover

Jesus Calling® for Little Ones
Board Book